Leadership …
Put a CAP on It!

Leadership …
Put a CAP on It!

◆

Become a Better Leader by Improving Your Communication, Attitude, and Performance

Benny T. Hughes

Edited by
Brandi L. Gallimore

iUniverse, Inc.
New York Bloomington Shanghai

Leadership ... Put a CAP on It!
Become a Better Leader by Improving Your Communication, Attitude, and Performance

iUniverse books may be ordered through booksellers or by contacting:

iUniverse
1663 Liberty Drive
Bloomington, IN 47403
www.iuniverse.com
1-800-Authors (1-800-288-4677)

Because of the dynamic nature of the Internet, any Web addresses or links contained in this book may have changed since publication and may no longer be valid.

The views expressed in this work are solely those of the author and do not necessarily reflect the views of the publisher, and the publisher hereby disclaims any responsibility for them.

ISBN: 978-0-595-47616-9 (pbk)
ISBN: 978-0-595-91881-2 (ebk)

Printed in the United States of America

To Judy and Jerry Koontz

Contents

Acknowledgments

First, I would like to thank and acknowledge my parents, Colon and Grace Hughes, for loving, supporting, and believing in me. I love you both! Special thanks to my sister, Colleen, for being my best friend and a great sister. Through the good and bad times, she has been there for me. I respect her more than I can express with words. I want to thank my brother, Frank, for his support, friendship, and the bond we share.

I would also like to acknowledge three people I miss dearly: Tony, my youngest brother, as well as my uncles, Johnnie and Evert. Even though they are not with us anymore, they impacted my life significantly. I think of them often.

I would like to thank and acknowledge Jerry and Judy Koontz for their influence and guidance through my life. You guys rock!

I am very grateful to Brandi Gallimore for her dedication, hard work, support, and the many outstanding suggestions she shared with me during the editing process of this book.

Special thanks to Wade Johnson and Jacquelin Houston for their friendship, mentorship, and leadership. They also provided a sounding board for many of the ideas in this text.

I really would like to thank the following people for their support and encouragement: Janeth Bean, Richard Beck, Brenda Bethune, Cathy Johnson, Demika Patterson, Greg Small, Jeff Gallimore, Lacy Cagle, Phil Rapp, Cherry Surratt, and Wilma White. Each has inspired and motivated me to be a better person and leader.

I feel very fortunate to have been associated with many wonderful people throughout my life. It is not possible to mention everyone who has impacted my life either on a personal or professional level. I sometimes realized the impact immediately, but I would not understand the positive effect of others until years later. This group of individuals includes family members, classmates, friends, and the many people I have worked with over the years. Thank you all!

I am very grateful to Carina Williams for providing me the confidence to write this book.

Introduction

Leadership ... Put a CAP on it. What does leadership mean? A very commonly used word, it is also a simple, yet traditionally powerful statement. Some people make it seem like it has magical powers when they use it. For instance, if a business has a very profitable year, it will often be attributed to the leadership of the CEO or chairperson. In another example, if a country's economy is booming and interest rates are down, it is frequently said that the president is displaying remarkable leadership.

At other times, leadership can be viewed as the reason for failure. Take the previous example. If the same company's performance is faltering, the blame is often shifted to the CEO's lack of leadership. Also, if a county's economy is suffering through a recession, the president's leadership is criticized and questioned.

Leaders, including schoolteachers as well as civilian and military leaders, have surrounded me for the past forty years. Of those leaders, the ones that I try to emulate are the ones who instilled a sense of direction and purpose in my life, whether at work or in my personal life.

So what is the difference between good and weak leadership? Effective leadership provides a sense of direction and purpose that motivates us to accomplish our goals. On the other hand, weak leadership often provides or suggests a goal but lacks direction and motivation to help us to accomplish that goal. Good leadership is not a cure-all. Leadership is broad and fluid. Therefore, a person cannot use a specific road map to become a good leader.

Effective leadership does consist of solid pillars, including communication, attitude, and performance. Therefore, I often tell audiences that they can improve their leadership by putting a "CAP" on their leadership style. Of course, as in most things, that is easier said than done, but I will explain throughout the text.

Communication

If leadership is to be useful and productive, good communication is a must. Leadership cannot exist without solid communication. If you examine any successful organization, including a small school's PTA or one of the largest companies in the world, one common denominator is that both organizations have a very meaningful communication structure. The notion of communication seems simple, but it sometimes seems so complex. In other words, it is simple when it works. However, other things fall short when communication fails.

For example, I was once watching a baseball game on TV. A ball was hit in the air. It initially appeared that the second baseman was going to easily catch the ball, but, at the last moment, the right fielder collided with him, causing the ball to fall to the ground. Immediately, the commentators pointed out how a routine play turned into a disaster because of the lack of communication between the two men. If the second baseman had caught the ball, no one would have probably even thought about communication being a part of the play.

One of the easiest ways for a leader to fail is to think that effective communication is a simple process and birthright. Being successful in the communication process requires desire, hard work, and determination.

Attitude

One's attitude, not aptitude, determines his or her altitude. When it comes to being successful, attitude cannot be underestimated. More than any other trait, a person's attitude can be the great equalizer in his or her success. Some people do not seem to be as talented as their co-workers, but they are more successful. Upon further review, I think you will discover that they possess a great attitude, giving them a certain edge. Consider Larry Bird. Compared to many of his counterparts in the NBA, he did not possess great athletic prowess. However, he will be forever mentioned as one of the greatest professional basketball players ever to play the game. Most would say it is because of his winning and determined attitude.

Performance

Outstanding performance is something that is expected, but it is sometimes harder to describe. A leader must ensure the mission is met.

But how is performance measured? Ideally, we have tools such as checklists, charts, and inspections that help us decide if performance is at the level it should be. However, a leader must often decide on the level of performance of his or her team without tools. While this is not easy, it can be done with the right focus, feedback, and vision.

Speakers or writers will regularly use anecdotes to make their point and teach. Throughout the text, you will find many stories and examples from my family and friends, as well as from famous people. It is my hope that these stories and examples will make for interesting and enjoyable reading. Also, by using this approach, I hope I will help you commit the lessons learned to memory.

PART I
Communication

1

Leadership Begins with Communication

Just as valuable as good location is to real estate or air is to breathing, communication is essential to successful leadership. Without good, valuable communication, strong or useful leadership simply does not occur.

A few years ago, I moved from one organization to another. My new office was equipped with a computer desk and a file cabinet. In the corner was a tall armoire with a heavy-duty lock lying on top. After further examination, I realized the key was missing. I searched over all the office, but I was unsuccessful. I asked the secretary and others whether they knew where the key was, but no one did. After staring at the heavy-duty lock for a couple days, I decided to just throw it away. Beyond being a paperweight, it had no value to me. A few days after throwing it away, I received an envelope with the key from our secretary. I am not sure what caused the delay in the key's delivery, but it was clear to me that I had been a victim of poor communication. This story illustrates that communication is imperative to effective leadership. Without solid communication, all leadership is a vehicle without any value.

How can a leader ensure that communication is valuable? One must make sure certain parameters and questions are answered. The leader must secure the organization's faith in his or her knowledge. The leader must also ensure that he or she is capable of leading the organization toward its goals. This rule applies at all levels. Whether a person is a supervisor of a two-person team or is leading a company of thousands, one must have credibility. Without establishing credibility, members will not be motivated to trust, believe, or put the extra effort needed to make an organization successful.

Establishing Credibility

As a leader, how can one establish credibility? In many cases, one assumes it initially by title or position. However, this does not mean it will last forever. Long-term credibility is not a birthright and should not be treated as such. Credibility should not be confused with authority or responsibility. Authority and responsibility are often associated with position or title. In many cases, they are organizationally or institutionally based. Credibility is earned, so based on individual actions and responses to situations, it can also be lost. To establish continuing credibility, a leader must be trusted because trust and credibility are synonymous. Trust begins with one being true to his or her word. In other words, say what you mean and mean what say. A credible leader ensures his or her words and actions create a record of trust.

In June 1981, I was preparing to enlist in the United States Air Force. I remember vividly a conversation I had with my father. He came into my room, carrying a small plaque.

My dad said, "I'm proud of your decision. I'm confident you'll do very well." He paused and then continued, "Your words and actions will be scrutinized initially to see if you can be trusted."

Next, he handed me the plaque. Our last name, Hughes, was printed in bold letters. Below our name, the following words were inscribed:

> You got it from your father; it was all he had to give. So it's yours to use and cherish for as long as you may live. If you lose the watch he gave you, it can be replaced. But a black mark on your name, my son, can never be erased. It was clean the day you took it and a worthy name to bear. When he got it from his father, there was no dishonor there. So make sure you guard it wisely after all is said and done. You'll be glad the name is spotless when you give it to your son.

My dad said, "Ensure that your word is your bond in every transaction you are involved in … both small and large."

He explained, "If your word is doubted, you are forcing other people to decide if you are telling the truth and can be trusted. Your trustworthiness should never be left up to debate. Always remember that a person's value to any organization, personal or professional, is based on his or her credibility."

Over the years, that conversation with my dad has remained with me. That plaque hangs in my office today.

Showing You Care

A saying goes, "People do not care how much you know until they know how much you care." As a leader, illustrating you care will aid you immensely with supervisors, peers, and subordinates. Try getting to know people on a personal level. Sending birthday, anniversary, and sympathy cards is very simple yet meaningful. Talking to team members about their hobbies and interests is more personal.

If you only discuss current or future work issues, it would be easy for people to conclude that you are concerned solely with the company or mission.

People often ask, "Which is more important, the people or the mission/company?"

The best answer would be, "Mission/company first, and people always."

Knowing people on a personal level does take time, but people on all different levels are motivated. They truly appreciate the idea of their leadership caring about them and their personal needs. When people know that someone cares about them, they will put out the extra effort to succeed. Some people may say, "I have to respect their position, but I do not have to respect them." In other words, one must do a good job for his or her leaders, but he or she will not do a great job unless he or she respects their leadership qualities.

As a leader, you will likely face a situation that someone in your organization will encounter a crisis in their personal life, including serious car accidents, suicides, deaths in the family, or many other serious incidents. First and foremost, people view themselves as fathers, mothers, sons, or daughters. Depending on the individual's priorities and values, he or she decides what else is important to him or her. Communicating during a crisis in an organization is hard for everyone involved. Support is the key during any difficult time, especially when a person is experiencing a personal tragedy. When leaders show compassion, empathy, concern, and patience, their actions speak volume. In most instances, this behavior will be deeply appreciated throughout the workplace. Actions, not just words, are the true indication of support.

When considering how to show people that you care for them on a personal level, realize that different people respond to different vehicles of motivation. Family members are great examples of this. Consider the following. While I was living in California, my sister and her husband brought their boys to visit me during their vacation. Their trip included stays in San Francisco, Vandenberg Air Force Base (where I lived), and San Diego. They took in many great sights like Yosemite National Park and the San Diego Zoo.

After returning to their home in North Carolina, my sister asked the boys, "What did you enjoy the most about the vacation?"

The youngest said, "I enjoyed the stay at Benny's house the best."

Not expecting that response, my sister asked, "What do you mean?"

He explained, "The gopher holes and Juicy Fruit."

Where I lived, there were lots of gophers that routinely dug up my yard. My nephew helped me locate the gophers' tunnels to cover their entrances and water the grass. Knowing my nephew liked chewing gum, I purchased him a package with ten individual packs of Juicy Fruit. While my sister, her husband, and their other son were having fond memories of Yosemite National Park and the San Diego Zoo, he was thinking about Juicy Fruit and gopher holes. This is one example of how people are motivated differently. Find what gopher holes work for people, and dig them through to success.

2

Leadership Traits

Leaders communicate and display their own personal and professional traits. Actions speak louder than words. Team members are observing and judging their leaders, basing their analysis on how their leaders responded in certain situations. In most cases, subordinates want their leaders to succeed. People enjoy being a part of a strong and productive organization. They realize the strength of an organization rests within the leadership. When a leader proves he or she possesses traits like vision, decisiveness, confidence, courage, and loyalty, others will want to follow.

A Leader's Vision

As a leader, one is expected to have a vision for the organization. You are expected to portray that vision throughout the organization. People want to follow someone who knows where he or she is going. More importantly, they want to know why their leader is taking that specific route. During all types of political elections, candidates are always explaining their vision. Often, these visions are considered to be broad and lacking in substance. However, that is not always the case.

Presidents Kennedy and Reagan were known as leaders with visions. President Kennedy challenged us to send humans to the moon; President Reagan promised to put an end to the Cold War. Although these seemed broad at the time, both dreams were achieved.

How does a leader explain his or her vision in a way that others will accept and follow? A vision should be simple to understand and attainable through dedication and hard work. Simplicity is key when getting others to accept and pursue a goal. For example, consider when a person is ill and sees his or her doctor. In most cases, the doctor has a greater understanding of the illness than the patient has. However, the patient is likely to follow the doctor's advice if the doctor simplifies his or her explanation to the point where the patient understands the premise of the illness and believes he or she will receive a benefit by following this advice.

Most visionary leaders are bold in that they are not afraid of change. President Kennedy discussed putting people on the moon when some thought it was far-fetched or even stupid. His courage to stay with his convictions changed the world as it was known.

A solid leader realizes that leadership environment is fluid. You must look for ways to constantly improve the workplace.

A Leader's Decisiveness

Effective leaders must make tough decisions and live with them. Several years ago, I had a supervisor who was an awesome person but had glaring weaknesses as a leader. It was very difficult for him to make a hard decision. He wanted to favor both sides and tried to give people things that were incompatible with what they needed. Good leaders realize there is a method to making tough choices. First, gather all of the facts, not just the favorable ones. If a leader makes a quick or reflex decision without knowing the facts, it will be hard for others to have faith in his or her decision-making process. Feedback from data and others is vital in the decision-making process.

Before making decisions, think about the advantages and disadvantages of each decision. While hindsight might be perfectly clear, thinking ahead and weighing the cost of the decision is a fundamental concept that cannot be over-looked during contemplation. A logical person would not think of making a sig-nificant purchase or taking a vacation without first thinking of how that decision would impact him or her as well as family members in the future.

The same principles hold true in an organization. Once a decision is made, one needs to move on and believe that the choice made is the right one. He or she must give time for the results to come to fruition.

In baseball, one often says, "A pitcher needs to trust his stuff." When the game is on the line and the decision has been made, rather than concerning himself with the thought that the correct pitch was selected, the pitcher should concen-trate on executing the pitch that was called. The same thought process should apply with making any decision. Decide, execute, and move on!

A Leader's Confidence

A communicative leader has confidence in his or her ability. He or she can trans-mit confidence throughout an organization. Recently, I decided I wanted to skydive. While I really wanted to do it, I was apprehensive. In other words, I was scared half to death!

I thought, "Thirteen thousand feet is a long way to fall. What if that parachute does not open up? What if I freeze up?"

After talking to my friend Ross, who has made more than thirty-two hundred successful jumps, and meeting the jumpmaster, my fears resided. Their confidences in the safety procedures and my ability to make a successful jump caused my thought process to transition from apprehension and fear to excitement and anticipation.

If a leader is viewed with having confidence in his or her abilities and the organization's goals, that confidence will turn into action for those following. President Reagan was extremely effective at instilling confidence throughout the nation in his ideas. He seemed to have so much confidence in himself with his ideas and plans. He was also an expert at communicating his ideas, so others believed his ideas were sound and worthwhile.

As a productive leader, one must remember that confidence has no value if a person is not able to put it into action for the organization. Confidence without action is often viewed as personal arrogance.

A Leader's Courage

I once asked a major in the air force, "What trait do you want a leader to have?"

Without hesitation, he said, "I want them to be more concerned about being right than being popular."

Possessing the courage to say no when everyone else is saying yes or turning right when the crowd wishes to turn left is not easy. It is especially difficult if the decision comes at a high personal cost for the leader or organization. Courage is a trait that most leaders think they posses.

One person might say, "I will tell it like it is." Another person might say, "Do not ask me a question unless you want the blunt truth."

In reality, many leaders choose to make popular or safe choices. People generally have a desire to be liked. They do not wish to engage in conflict if it can be avoided. Also, it is very easy to rationalize one's opinion so it appears that he or she used good judgment and were not persuaded by peer or institutional pressure. Making tough decisions can be difficult. It can sometimes make a leader unpopular.

A brave leader must have the courage to make the decision that he or she thinks is best for the organization. Then he or she must learn how to live with that decision. While the leader will not always be right concerning his or her decisions and the bottom line, he or she will be respected throughout the organization if he or she possesses the courage to go with his or her convictions.

A Leader's Loyalty

Leaders must exhibit loyalty to their subordinates, peers, and superiors in their organization. For members of any organization to be comfortable, they must feel they can count on their leadership to represent their best interests.

Even though being loyal and pleasing people can be different, they are often associated as one. From a leader's standpoint, loyalty is viewed as being faithful in decisions and treatment. There will be times when a leader's loyalty is tested.

Consider when a leader has been selected or promoted to a position within the same organization. In some cases, that person could be supervising his or her previous peers. In this somewhat uncomfortable environment, subordinates, peers, and superiors in the institution will scrutinize the leader's actions to see if he or she exhibits a bias. The leader will be tested to see how he or she adjusts to the new position. If this occurs, the leader must ensure that he or she stays focused and does not get caught up in the personal situation.

Leadership is broad. It should not be reduced to a focus on what is personal. If a leader allows his or her personal loyalty to a group of people or a person to become the main point in his or her decision-making process, he or she will often make a choice that is not healthy for the organization as a whole. While it is natural and admirable to not want to disappoint anyone, a leader must realize that his or her first loyalty is to doing the right thing and making the right decision for everyone concerned in the organization. If a leader views loyalty on an institutional level instead of the personal level, it will be more beneficial and productive for the end result of the organization.

3

Two-way Communication Is the Only Way

One-way streets can often be confusing and frustrating. The same can be said about one-way communication. A leader should not expect blind obedience from members in his or her organization. When I was a kid, I watched the popular TV sitcom *Gomer Pyle* with Jim Nabors as Private Gomer Pyle and Frank Sutton as Sergeant Vince Carter. Gomer was a simple, humble, good-hearted, goofy, and very lovable man from North Carolina. Sergeant Carter was a marine's marine. He was razor-sharp, tough, and intimidating. His job was to train and mold Private Pyle to be the same. The one-way method of communication that Sergeant Carter employed was based on the principle of blind obedience. If you watched the show, you know Sergeant Carter's method was ineffective in most cases. Private Pyle was an easygoing person. Even though he tried his hardest to succeed, he just was incapable of being effective and productive in a relationship where communication just went one way. Even though there are not many people like Private Pyle in the workplace, if one-way communication is typically used, it will yield the long-term result of less production and unmotivated workers.

For most people, it is not enough to just be a member of a successful organization. They want to contribute to the success of the organization, which is not possible unless two-way communication exists. It is the leader's key responsibilities to ensure the path of two-way communication is active in the organization. To do this, ensure members are allowed input and involvement concerning the communication or objective that one is presenting.

Two of my favorite teachers were Mr. and Mrs. Koontz. Mrs. Koontz taught science in junior high; Mr. Koontz was my high school history teacher. Even though I had many outstanding teachers, something was different about the approach that these two employed. Not only were they teachers, they were role models, mentors, and leaders as well. I did not realize what was different about their tactics until several years after I graduated high school and became an instructor myself. Both Mr. and Mrs. Koontz knew how to make each student feel as if he or she were part of the lesson. Sometimes, they would do this with a question or an example that might include students in a skit or reenactment. Whatever method they used, they ensured that each student felt involved in the lesson. By doing this, it encouraged the students to feel active and integrated in the communication that was taking place.

If a member of an organization feels as if he or she is actually part of what is happening, he or she will be more likely to participate in the communication cycle. As an individual, he or she may feel that he or she is helping to reach the organization's objectives. In many cases, when an individual feels personal involvement in the communication, he or she will not hesitate to voice his or her own concerns and ideas.

When it comes to the organization's goals, input and involvement in the communication process will often prompt acceptance from an individual. It is a human response to want leaders to hear concerns and thoughts. But most people realize a decision has to be made. While they might not agree with the decision in whole, they can accept and support it when they and others in the organization had the opportunity to give input.

Be Careful When Your Hands Are Talking

While communicating on a personal level is great, it often is not a viable method. Communicating organizationally is paramount as well. E-mails can be very effective ways of communicating to large groups of people at once. However, there are some rights and wrongs with using e-mails. E-mail works great for disseminating general information like policy changes and trends that employees should be aware of. However, there are times when the use of e-mail seems too indirect.

When possible, you should never transmit anger or tremendous disappointment over e-mail. It is very easy to type words that are hurtful and do not express what you really mean. Also, because e-mail is a source of one-way communication, you may not have all of the details in many cases. If you think a situation could become emotional, it is more appropriate to have a one-on-one conversation. If face-to-face communication is not an option, then use the telephone.

Never use e-mail to give bad news to individuals or large groups. It can be devastating for a person to find out that he or she did not get a position or he or she is losing a job over an e-mail. News like this should always be done in an environment where one can explain and answer questions.

Sympathy, empathy, and true concern cannot easily be transmitted through e-mail. Do not use it when you can use your feet. Get out from behind the desk. Go out and visit folks. If you have information that impacts a large number of people, then call a staff meeting or conduct a seminar. While circulation of information is a must, an effective leader must realize that e-mail does not have eyes, ears, and a heart. It does not show a deep concern for people.

Newsletters, either electronic or on paper, are another effective way of communicating within an organization. Information such as promotions, retirements, birthdays, wedding anniversaries, and birth announcements can be announced through newsletters. Articles from the organization leadership on their thoughts and concerns often enlighten and build confidence throughout the workplace. Newsletters are often published regularly, depending on the size and structure of the organization.

Communicating with Your Ears

When encouraging opinions from others in the workplace, the leader must listen to concerns from team members. Being an effective listener is not easy for most people. It requires much effort and desire to master the mechanics of listening. Many people, including leaders, listen for their thoughts to be confirmed rather than listening to confirm others. They are listening to ensure that their own thoughts and desires are understood and will be acted on. Once those desires are confirmed, they are ready to move on to the next subject.

How can you tell if a leader is listening to be confirmed rather than to confirm? He or she often interrupts others while they are talking. The leader's interruption would not necessarily be a sign of being rude. It is a reaction of him or her concluding that his or her desires are more important, so he or she feels no need to hear any more information concerning other opinions. This behavior would be detrimental in trying to create an environment where others thought their input should be valued.

Effective leaders listen because they are genuinely concerned, not because they are required to listen. How can you tell when someone is only listening out of necessity? One example of this is when a leader will listen intently to his or her superiors. However, when they are listening to their peers or subordinates, they act as they have an earache. If subordinates or peers think a leader only listens to superiors, the leader runs the risk of being labeled as someone who is only concerned about personal advancement. He or she does not want to obtain the best results for the organization.

Also consider when a leader only listens to topics that impact him or her. If a leader is not concerned, he or she will be perceived as uncaring. Good leaders realize that listening is a process that cannot be turned on and off at convenience.

Listen intently to every theory as if it could be the next great idea. This will have a positive impact on the organization. Listening with concern will create an environment so that followers will seek out their leader, providing their ideas to get feedback.

Hearing takes time, but listening takes desire, time, and concentration. Not only does listening consist of hearing the communication, it also includes processing it as well.

A while ago, I was watching a documentary focusing on producers of popular television shows.

One producer was asked, "What is one of the most difficult parts of your job?"

He explained, "Trying to ensure the actors and actresses maintained a high level of concentration when they were listening to the instructions and advice they were given. That is the most difficult."

He further described, "In many cases, there were so many things going on at once. In order for an actor or actress to mentally process what he or she was told and react, it took a high level of concentration."

This is true for leaders as well. In many cases, a leader will have many different actions occurring simultaneously. One of the actions will often be a conversation with a member of the organization. It is paramount that one can shift his or her attention completely to that individual and comprehend what is being said.

For several years in the air force, I served as a first sergeant. As in many leadership positions, the duties of first sergeant is very broad and diverse. A first sergeant typically deals with an array of issues, ranging from speeding tickets to death notifications. Sometimes, several events of different levels of importance could occur within a five-minute period.

At first, the job's responsibility overwhelmed me. I had to listen with intense concentration. I did not want to miss a detail from a conversation that could change a decision that might impact a person and his or her family in a negative way. Because I was so concerned about not missing any details, I would often have headaches. One day in a conversation, I informed my squadron commander of this circumstance.

He advised me, "Concentrating on a conversation is a mind-set. A leader should treat every conversation like it was the most important conversation that he has engaged in that day."

By doing this, listening would become more routine and less stressful. The leader would be processing the information clearly to be able to make a good decision.

Listening to a person validates his or her importance to the organization. Leaders at all levels must ensure that all the members of the organization believe that their concerns and ideas will be considered. To ensure that this occurs, set the example when it comes to listening. If a leader listens to the members of the organization and the members sees results, they will often want to incorporate it into their leadership style.

If something works, most of us will be inclined to try it. This statement holds true with listening skills as well.

When I hear someone say nice things about his or her supervisor, I ask, "What makes your supervisor special?"

I frequently hear, "He cares about me and my work."

I then ask, "How do you know that your supervisor really has a concern for you and your efforts?"

The person usually responds, "He listens to me."

But listening to an idea does not always mean implementing it. Too often, people in leadership positions tend to stop listening once they think the idea will not be implemented. Leaders should listen to the whole idea with an open mind and a positive view. Most people realize that leaders will not act on all of their concerns, but they are content if they know that someone is taking time to listen with an open mind. If the listening process is utilized throughout an organization, that is a good indicator that communication is successful.

A common saying is "Keep it Simple, Sam" (or Samantha). This principle is also known as KISS. A leader can apply this standard to listening. To do this, do not overreact to the communication. If a leader yells unnecessarily, it often creates an environment where the organization is on edge and tense. A leader should listen intently for the entire message, not buzzwords like "difficult" or "costly." Some people may say, "It has never been done before." Oftentimes, buzzwords will cause a reflex action from a leader, which will complicate the communication process. Leaders can enhance the listening process simply by realizing that, like smiling, listening is contagious. If a leader listens with a smile whenever possible, others will react positively.

4

Confirming that Communication Exists

Questions are essential to the listening process. Questions that a leader asks can directly influence the conversation. Thought-provoking questions can add value and direction to the communication; questions that are disjointed or confusing can detract from the conversation or presentation.

One of the most influential people in my life was my Uncle Evert. Even though he passed away in 2003, I often think of the fond memories that we shared. We discussed both professional and personal situations that occurred in my life. I always felt better after talking with him. He would ask me questions that were the most appropriate and thought-provoking. Uncle Evert had a manner of giving me advice and guidance through questions. He could encourage, educate, support, confirm, and caution me in this manner. It was very uncommon for him to tell me not to do something or assert I had made a bad decision. I knew what guidance he was giving me based on the questions he asked. Like Uncle Evert, outstanding leaders ask good questions that add to the value of communication.

As with most things in life, timing is important when posing a question. A leader should ensure the speaker has finished his or her thought before asking a question. This is especially true when asking a tough follow-up question. The speaker needs ample time to explain his or her answer and know the leader is processing the message. Question-and-answer sessions should not seem like a tennis match between the leader and speaker.

Asking questions is not a contact sport, so it should not be treated as one. A leader's attitude is a chief component when posing a question. If a leader asks a question in a negative or combative fashion, it can impact the speaker's attitude. When possible, ask questions in a way that the individual does not feel like he or she is on trial for committing a crime.

Consider the following example of a combative question. Someone may ask, "Can you please tell me why we need to waste another five thousand dollars toward the break room renovation project?"

Instead, it is better to ask this neutral question: "Could you please explain why we need to increase the break room renovation budget by five thousand dollars?"

Leaders' questions should be viewed as both clarified and positive reinforcement tools, so the leader's attitude is the main ingredient.

Seeing Is Believing

Communication in an organization is a simple process when it works, but it is complex to deploy. How does a leader know the communication process in his or her organization is being put into motion? One indicator is that "seeing is believing." Leaders should focus on the mood of their organizations. If people are pleased with their organization's communication, their action will indicate it. They will talk more, laugh more, and be more focused on their work.

Several years ago, I attended a conference in St. Louis with a close friend. One evening, we went to dinner at a very nice restaurant. After we were seated, I noticed my friend kept looking over in the corner of the dining area.

I asked, "What's catching your attention?"

She said, "There's a young couple sitting in the corner of the room."

When I looked over and spotted them, they appeared to be in their twenties.

My friend asked, "Do you notice anything different about them?"

I said, "They look to be having a great time and are really in tune with each other."

During dinner, we both kept noticing how the young couple stood out from all of the others in the restaurant. While everyone seemed to be enjoying themselves and their dinner, something was different about these young people. They seemed to be enjoying themselves on a much higher level than everyone else in the room was. The young couple even appeared to have a special glow about them. After dinner, as we were leaving the restaurant, the young couple passed by us.

My friend commented, "You look so happy together."

The young lady explained, "We just got engaged, and we're celebrating the happy occasion."

Just like the young couple's happiness, great communication will be evident when present. If outstanding communication is present in an organization, it will be apparent by people's actions and how relaxed, yet motivated, they are.

Recognition Sends a Strong Message

Institutionally, people need to know that their efforts are appreciated. You can implement a solid recognition program. While waiting on my order at a fast-food restaurant, I saw a bulletin board with pictures of the employees of the month. When I turned to see if my order was ready, I noticed a young lady staring at me and smiling. I glanced back at the board and realized I was staring at her picture before.

I said, "Congratulations on your award."

She replied, "Thank you very much. I love it here. I have the best supervisor in the world."

She did not brag on how many hours she had worked or how many customers she had waited on. She was much more interested in letting me know that her leader appreciated her.

Recognition—or the lack of recognition—often sends a strong message of whether or not the organization values the efforts of its workers. Recognition and awards can include time off, monetary rewards, or plaques and trophies. However, it should be emphasized that recognition should be viewed as being as fair as possible. If recognition is not viewed as being just across diversity lines like gender, race, and age, it is useless and will do much more harm than good.

Solid recognition programs are competitive and based on merit. If recognition and awards programs are operated as round-robin tournaments, they will lack the muscle to motivate members of the organization.

The size of the recognition program is also important. It should be large enough to serve as a motivation tool, but it should be small enough that people are not being awarded for just showing up to work.

Ask and Receive

What is another way to ensure that communication is effective? Have mediums where others can voice their opinions as well. Feedback tools like hotlines, suggestion boxes, or critique forms are great ways to accomplish a communication flow. If an organization creates avenues for its people to outlet their concerns, this will enhance the organization's opportunity to gain accurate and sincere feedback from within. However, having communication feedback tools and not utilizing them is futile. It is paramount that members of an organization believe that the feedback mechanisms are in place to enhance the communication process realistically and they are not there just for show.

A logical person would not go on a trip if the gas gauge on his or her vehicle was not functioning correctly. He or she would not know how much fuel was in the tank. Communication is the fuel that propels leadership. Feedback tools should be in place to ensure the organization has an accurate understanding of how well communication is working within the institution.

Effective leadership begins and ends with good communication. No organization, big or small, can obtain success without healthy two-way communication. This communication must start with the leaders. In order for communication to be meaningful, leaders must be credible, confident, decisive, and loyal. A solid leader listens intently to subordinates, peers, and superiors, knowing that good ideas and thoughts are not limited to just one group of people. Questions by leaders, when properly constructed, can add value to the conversation. They are a must. Questions can support, motivate, caution, and endorse when used correctly. Communication in an organization must be visible and active. Finally, a leader should have feedback mechanisms in place to ensure that communication is productive in the workplace.

Leadership starts with communication. My first advice to you as a leader is to improve yourself in leadership by putting a *C* in your CAP and start becoming a more valuable leader.

PART II
Attitude

5

Attitude Determines Altitude

In the introduction, I stated that I believed attitude, not aptitude, determines one's altitude. No tool is more important to a leader than his or her attitude and the way that others perceive his or her mind-set. To others, you are what your attitude says you are. People are very comfortable following and trusting someone with a trustworthy attitude rather than someone who is extremely intelligent. Compared to intelligence and experience, attitude is a much more reliable indicator about an individual's leadership capabilities. Someone could be extremely bright and experienced, but others cannot trust him or her to lead. While a great attitude alone does not guarantee that a person will be a great leader, it is a perfect medium to enhance a leader's success.

Much like a rich salad dressing on a bed of lettuce, a good attitude can enhance a leader's effectiveness. A salad can consist of fresh vegetables and delicious meats, but if the dressing is not to a person's liking, he or she will likely pass on the offering.

Take that same salad with a dressing that is appealing to the taste buds, and you have the start of a great meal. A leader's attitude works in the same manner as the salad dressing. In many cases, if a leader has a lot of experience but exhibits an attitude that is overbearing, arrogant, and mean-spirited, he or she will alienate people, who will refuse to follow. But if the leader presents an attitude that others trust and enjoy, people will line up to support him or her.

What traits does a good attitude consist of? While there is no one recipe for describing the ingredients that comprise the perfect leader's attitude, some tendencies and thought processes will help a leader with developing an attitude that will improve his or her leadership style. These include being professional, committed, and passionate. Also, one should remain humble and not become complacent. These key ingredients will advance a leader's efficiency in his or her organization.

Being Viewed as a Professional

Being viewed as professional by others in a society is paramount. What makes one a professional? When I think of professionalism, people like Colin Powell, Peter Jennings, Tiger Woods, and Pat Summitt come to mind. All of these people, leaders in their profession, are—or were—extremely successful. But just being successful or in charge does not ensure one will be viewed as a professional. Being a professional is more about delivering who one is than what one is.

What traits does a professional possess? There is no exclusive skill set one must present before he or she is viewed as a professional. But certain behaviors can help a leader become a recognized and respected person who conducts himself or herself in a professional manner. Such behaviors include, but are not limited to, possessing a positive attitude, presenting appropriate dress and appearance, being articulate, showing patience, and reacting properly during stressful situations.

Possessing a positive attitude is an outstanding foundation in success. A leader cannot control most of the stresses that occur on a daily basis, but he or she can control his or her attitude. Leaders have a great opportunity to enhance the environment simply by attacking the goal with a professional, positive attitude. Of course, controlling individual attitude is a personal responsibility. One can accomplish that by being self-disciplined, surrounding oneself with positive people, or perhaps engaging in positive activities, such as reading a motivational text, exercising, and eating healthy. Adults often caution children on the danger of choosing the wrong friends and activities. This is good advice for children as well as adults and leaders because it impacts their attitude.

How can a leader create a positive work environment? First, present a positive attitude. For example, view a problem as an opportunity to achieve rather than a burden. Successful leaders know that there will be difficult challenges in their organization. They are responsible for creating an environment where their organization will succeed.

In 2004, during the American League Championship Series, the Boston Red Sox found themselves down three games to zero in the best of a seven-game series to the New York Yankees. No team in baseball history had come back from this type of deficit and won.

Boston's manager, Terry Francona, who was in his first year as the Boston skipper, was often asked, "How are you going to convince your team that they could win four straight and make it to the World Series?"

He replied that the Red Sox did not have to win four straight games. For them to keep their team's goals alive, they just had to win the next game.

Francona took a seemingly insurmountable problem and broke it down into a very attainable goal. Boston made baseball history by beating the Yankees and then winning their first World Series championship in eighty-six years.

Does dressing professionally actually make an individual smarter or make one a better leader? While dress and appearance might not increase one's IQ, it can definitely enhance how prepared and intelligent one is perceived to be. In 1960, more than seventy million viewers watched the first presidential debate ever to be televised between Senator John Kennedy and Vice President Richard Nixon. A knee injury had kept Vice President Nixon in the hospital for two weeks. He was twenty pounds underweight, and he arrived at the debate wearing a shirt that did not fit him well. Moreover, he refused makeup to improve his color. When Senator Kennedy arrived, he was tan, confident, and well-rested.

After the debate, the audience was surveyed for their thoughts. Those who had watched the debate on television felt Senator Kennedy had won the debate by a large margin. However, those who listened to the debate on the radio felt Vice President Nixon won by a slim margin.

While it is said that you cannot judge a book by it cover, leaders are not books. They are people. Judgments are often made on the professional image that a leader presents throughout the organization. If a person has the appearance of a professional, he or she will usually be treated as if he or she knows what he or she is doing until proven differently. However, if a person has the appearance of a slob, it will be very difficult for him or her to be viewed as an expert and a leader in his or her field. In many cases, people are seen before they have the chance to interact with their audience. Therefore, impressions are often based on appearance and actions. If the appearance is that of a professional, others will immediately treat the professional as a person who knows his or her trade.

Productive leaders are able to articulate a message to everyone in the organization. Having an idea is not enough. One must be able express his or her idea to others in a manner that everyone understands the thought process, concerns, and vision. The focus is on the leader to articulate his or her message. Leaders should carefully consider others' job knowledge, experience, and education level when choosing the words and methods when making their point of view. Effective leaders realize that one style of communication will not apply to every person in the organization. Leaders should articulate their message in a manner that is received as simple yet structured.

It is easy for a leader to lose his or her credibility through unprofessional lapses of judgment. You must ensure that your language is viewed as professional. While certain words can add spice or a point of emphasis to conversations or briefings, ensure that salty words and profanity do not offend anyone. Even though people may laugh or may not be offended at profanity, it is unwise to use it in a professional setting. Leaders should possess a full vocabulary in order to articulate their point of view without sprinkling in profane words or phrases that could offend others.

Exercise Patience to Speed the Process

While many successful leaders are aggressive in their approach to accomplish a mission, they must know when to exercise patience. A leader's patience will send the message that he or she has not given up and he or she realizes that effort alone does not guarantee results. Often, positive results follow trial and error as well as adjustments to be made in the process.

When I was eleven years old, I wanted to learn how to swim, but I was afraid. My grandfather offered to teach me. The idea of him teaching me scared me even more. Even though my grandfather was a great man and I was very close to him, he was not known for his patience. He would often yell and become upset if the results were not what he desired. However, I agreed and let him teach me how to swim.

He stood in water that was so deep that I could not have touched the bottom. I ran up to the edge of the pond several times and stopped short because I was terrified. Surprisingly, my grandfather never raised his voice. Instead, he kept encouraging me and telling me that he was proud of me. He also said he knew I would be a great swimmer.

Finally, after several failed attempts, I jumped in the water. When I came to the surface, I began to swim for the first time in my life. My grandfather's patience was the primary reason that I was able to succeed at a task I was unsure of doing.

If a leader is viewed as patient, he or she is often seen as approachable. Followers are not concerned about being viewed as a failure. Also, patient leaders are often viewed as people who are truly concerned and do not view others as just a resource.

Remaining Calm and Being Successful

Professionals in an organization are expected to remain calm and deliver results in stressful situations. Most people can smile and remain cool when things are good. However, when the environment turns stressful, most become shaken and incapable of leadership, including making good, solid decisions.

One of the most tragic and stressful times in United States history occurred on September 11, 2001. Because of the events of that day, people were frightened, angry, and disorganized. Most people wondered what was going to happen next. Most of us looked for direction from our country's leadership. While many great people performed unbelievably well during this tragedy, the mayor of New York City, Rudy Giuliani, gained many accolades and praise for his performance during the days and months after the events of September 11. His leadership style had a calming effect and added direction during a time of turmoil and confusion. I felt more secure after watching Mayor Giuliani's calm demeanor. He was poised, visible, and decisive. His style of leadership added a feeling of stability to the entire country during a time of tremendous crisis.

On a much smaller scale than September 11, every organization faces stressful situations. Members of the organization expect their leadership to lead and instill a calming effect on the organization.

Like Mayor Giuliani, all leaders need to be visible throughout their organizations during a time of crisis. When a leader is visible, it proves he or she is involved and personally knows what events are occurring. Also, it is paramount that the leader has a plan. He or she should make the plan known within the organization. In a time of high stress and crisis, people are looking for direction and hope. While it is impossible for anyone to make the right decisions every time, especially in a stressful environment, people want to know that their leader can react to a high-stress situation without overreacting or making decisions based on panic or fear.

6

Stay Focused with Commitment, Determination, and Passion

Commitment is the core of a person's attitude. Without an attitude of true commitment, success will not occur. For example, if you look at any accomplished lawyer, doctor, athlete, businessperson, military leader, or educator, I promise it will be obvious that the person is committed to his or her vision, mission, and goals.

One example of extreme commitment is President Abraham Lincoln. He ran for Congress three times before he won, only to lose when he was up for reelection. He also suffered defeats in two runs for the Senate and a run for vice president. President Lincoln realized that commitment was the key to success. He never gave up, and he stayed committed to his beliefs.

Effective leadership requires commitment. In addition, solid leaders must understand that there is a huge difference between involvement and commitment. For example, a huge wedding requires involvement from many key participants, including the wedding party, photographer, preacher, florist, friends, and family. However, while all of the aforementioned people are heavily involved in the wedding ceremony, the only two who must be truly committed to a successful and happy marriage are the two who are getting married. If the bridal couple is just involved, but not committed to each other, the marriage will likely be short-lived. Being truly committed is often much less attractive than simply being involved. Commitment is a true way of showing belief in something or somebody, even when it is difficult.

Leaders must be committed to their organization. When discussing organization commitment, it can be broken down into two categories: institutional and people. Institutional commitment includes supporting the organization's goals, policies, and vision. Commitment to people includes compensation, fair treatment, and advancement.

Institutional Commitment

All companies and organizations have goals. Successful leaders are concerned and committed to achieving the goals.

When I was growing up, my grandfather used to ask me frequently, "What are you going to do tomorrow?"

I would often reply, "I don't know."

He would respond, "You should know, Benny! How do you expect anything good to happen if you don't have a plan or a goal?"

An effective leader realizes that favorable results just do not occur without sweat, equity, and brainpower. A solid leader understands that he or she must support and enforce organizational policies. Policies such as dress code, breaks, and work schedules must be strictly followed. Others in the organization view a leader in order to gauge personal commitment to the organization. If a person in charge walks by a violation without correcting it, he or she is endorsing that act. By not correcting the violation, the leader is essentially saying that the rule is silly. Most know that actions speaks louder than words. If a leader supports something in a staff meeting or signs a policy letter, yet does not abide by or enforce the policies with his or her actions, it will not be long until others challenge his or her institutional commitment. Thus the leader will lose credibility.

It is paramount that leaders support their organization's vision. While goals are what one plans to achieve, vision is how they are achieved. One way of doing this is to suggest certain ideals and a direction that the organization should go in. While a leader must be concerned about the short-term outlook, he or she must realize that he or she has a responsibility to the long-term future of the organization as well. Most parents do not suggest to their children that they enroll in the easiest course in high school because they know this would be damaging to the child's long-term success. The same principle applies within the workplace. A leader must be thinking about both short- and long-term success.

What if there are instances when a leader does not agree with an organization's goals, policies, or vision? The leader has the responsibility to voice concerns of his or her personal beliefs to management. This is easier said than done. Often, disagreeing with institutional thinking creates a tense environment. Sometimes superiors might question the leader's commitment. This situation demands that one make one's case in an objective manner. The best approach in this case is to state the facts as you understand them and remain calm.

In the end, a leader must understand that the organization's beliefs are more important than personal opinions and should support his or her organization's decisions. This is always true unless a leader feels the organization's views are illegal, immoral, or to the point that he or she cannot support them with a clear conscience. In that case, the leader can either voice his concerns to other venues or leave the organization entirely. While neither of these choices is easy, good leaders understand their commitment to the organization is very important. The situation must be treated in a manner that commitment to the organization is honored if possible.

Organization's Commitment to Individuals

Despite race, gender, and age lines, fair treatment is expected. It is the responsibility of everyone in the organization. Even though everyone shares this responsibility, the actual enforcement is the responsibility of the leadership. Usually, the organization handles the management of discrimination policies and violations. The organization considers the involvement of the responsible parties as a personal matter of the highest degree. Leaders must ensure that active processes enable everyone in the organization to voice his or her concerns about any unfair treatment. An organization's morale can be directly linked to how fair the workplace is. To add more responsibility, a leader's effectiveness can be a result of how he or she is enforcing and maintaining fairness inside the organization.

Advancement in life is something that most people take very seriously. That same seriousness holds true in the workplace. But advancement is a broad term, and it does not have the same meaning for everyone. To some, advancement is mostly about pay increases. To others, it is about increased responsibilities and status that come with a promotion. Some may feel like advancing is linked to increasing their job knowledge. While people within organizations describe advancement differently, most believe it is the leadership's responsibility to ensure it is available as well as fair. An environment perceived to have little or no room for advancement makes it highly likely that workers will become bored and lose their edge.

What can a leader do to ensure advancement is available for his or her followers? First, make sure an environment exists where others believe that hard work is expected as well as appreciated and will be rewarded. Leaders should be aware of the workers short- and long-term goals. They should also know their strengths and weakness. Then they should work with employees to improve job performance. Improvement in job performance will set the foundation for advancement within the organization when the opportunity presents itself.

Determination Comes from Within

Determination is the fuel that drives commitment. Every day, I try to live by the following phrase, "If your ship does not come in, then swim out to meet it." Determination to succeed when failure appears to be certain is not easy, and it takes inner strength. Glenn Cunningham is an outstanding example of this. In 1916, at the age of seven, he nearly died in a schoolhouse fire that took his brother's life. Cunningham's legs were burned so badly that his doctor initially thought it would be necessary to amputate them. It was possible that he might never have walked again. But he endured the terrible pain. After several months of exercise, he was able to stand on his own. After a year, he was able to walk.

Cunningham would later say, "By the grace of God, I learned to run again."

Not only did he run again, he became one of the greatest track stars of his time. During the 1934 Olympics in Los Angeles, he finished fourth in the 1500-meter race. The next year, he received the prestigious Sullivan Award as the country's top amateur athlete. He also won the silver medal in the 1936 Berlin Olympics.[1]

Solid leaders realize that life has no panacea. In order to be successful and accomplish goals, one must not give up. It sounds simple to say that you are not going to give up, but it is actually one of the toughest challenges a person can face. Staying focused and determined to achieve a goal will test an individual's moral fiber. Often, what makes staying determined so difficult is the fact that maintaining the course does not guarantee success. The key to determination is to believe that you can accomplish the goal and that it is worth the effort and resources that it takes to do so.

President Lincoln is widely credited with saying, "Always bear in mind that your own resolution to succeed is more important than any one thing."[2]

While a leader's determination comes from within, it can impact his or her surroundings. Glenn Cunningham's determination impacted the history of the Olympics. A person never knows how his or her individual will to succeed will impact others and the future of the organization.

Passion Proves Your Purpose

To achieve in life, we must care about what we are doing. So, to take it a step further, in order to truly succeed, one must truly care. Therefore, if a leader wants

1. Kansas Sports Hall of Fame, "Cunningham, Glenn V." *Hall of Famers.* http://www.kshof.org/hof-profiles.cfm?record_id=12.
2. Quoted on Matthew Doucette's official Web site, "Inspirational Quotes," http://www.matthewdoucette.com/inspirationalquotes/.

to really succeed, he or she must really care about what he or she is doing. Caring is a verb and is proven by action. Sustaining action takes passion. A person's energy and passion keep him or her pushing forward, believing the effort will be worthwhile.

I often ask people, "How long do you plan to do a certain job or a task?"

In many cases, they simply answer, "Until I stop having fun."

While I believe in what they say, I think the most specific and accurate answer is, "Until I lose the passion for what I am doing."

It is very hard to have fun in a job if there is a lack of passion for the task.

Passion is more about energy and delivery than the act itself. Passion is personal. I really enjoy watching and listening to Joel Osteen, a popular minister. On many occasions, I have heard him tell stories and read scriptures that I have heard many times before. However, he does it with such enthusiasm that I say, "Wow! That is great! Tell me more!" Not only do passionate leaders care, they motivate others through their passion and desire to be successful.

How do leaders motivate others through their passion? They must set the example. On a recent trip, I decided to have lunch in between meetings. I was trying to decide on what to have. I was in an area where several restaurants were available. Suddenly, I smelled pizza that smelled good. I noticed the pizza stand, and I went to take a closer look. A young lady with a huge smile greeted me.

I said, "Hello, you seem in a great mood today."

She smiled really wide and said, "I am having a great day. You will, too, after you have a piece of our pizza."

Before she asked for my order, she explained how their pizza was always hot and fresh. She told me how they prepared the pizza and how their ovens were better than most. During the entire conversation, she was smiling and talking enthusiastically. After witnessing her passion, I could not wait to try a piece of pizza. She was correct! The pizza was terrific. After I finished my lunch, I thought about how impressed I was with the young woman and her attitude. Her passion motivated me for the rest of the day.

The organization's actions can influence an individual's passion. It is the leader's job to ensure that the workplace environment is one that is high in job satisfaction. No one can be excited if he or she is not satisfied. I know it sounds elementary, but it is more complex than simply linking the words "excited" and "satisfied" together. The person in charge must understand what adds to job satisfaction and what his or her responsibilities are to foster an environment where members throughout the organization experience job satisfaction.

Ensure that pride exists in your organization. Pride is something that most desire in all aspects of life. Whether it is in our families, on the golf course, or at work, humans want to feel like they accomplished something good and they feel at peace while doing it.

In addition to job satisfaction, leaders should also strive to foster an environment where members throughout the organization have pride in their work. To do this, create a workplace environment that is stable and consistent. The requirements for stability and consistency in the work environment include everything from standard expectations, such as lighting and room temperature, to broader expectations, such as healthy interpersonal relationships and organizational accomplishments.

7

Pride, Excellence, and Humility

Pride, like commitment, can be broken into two categories: organizational and individual. Organizational pride exhibits pride in the company itself. My father worked in the textile industry for thirty years. Needless to say, he was very proud of his company. Anytime he had an opportunity, he would make approving comments about Burlington Industries. He was proud of their product, and he was proud to be a part of their institution.

Individual pride relates to an individual's contributions to his or her organization. In the early 1980s, "Inspector 12" ads were all over television. Inspector 12, an older, very stern lady, would inspect Hanes underwear and stamp "Inspected by 12" on them. Then she would comment, "They don't say Hanes until I say they say Hanes!"

Individual pride hinges on the theme that the quality of "my" work represents who I am. Most people want to feel that they are part of something much larger than themselves. This can occur when an individual realizes his or her contribution will help in the organization's success.

Just as leaders must realize what adds to an individual's pride or satisfaction in his or her work, they must be aware of what actions do not increase pride or job satisfaction. Often, it is thought that salary is the key component to job satisfaction. But multiple surveys completed over the years suggest salary is actually far down the list when it comes giving someone job satisfaction. Salary is more often viewed as necessary rather than satisfying.

My friend Jeff Gallimore was once asked, "How much money does someone have to make to live comfortably in your area?"

Jeff smiled and responded, "The amount of money that they make."

Jeff had a good point. He meant that, in most cases, workers' living standards are what they can afford and are viewed as requirements.

Strive for Excellence

Successful leaders strive for excellence and do not accept mediocrity. Henry Ford described the race for excellence as, "The best we can do is size up the chances, calculate the risks involved, estimate our ability to deal with them and then make our plans with confidence."[1] Obviously, Henry Ford did not accept mediocrity from himself or inside of his organization.

So how does a leader develop the attitude of excellence to ensure his or her organization does not fall into mediocrity? Aristotle once said, "Excellence is an art won by training and habituation. We do not act rightly because we have virtue or excellence; rather, we have those because we have acted rightly; we are what we repeatedly do. Excellence, then, is not an act but a habit."[2] When you take these statements from Henry Ford and Aristotle and tie them together, you have a great recipe for the pursuit of excellence in any organization. Leaders should ensure that their organization has a mind-set that is conducive to the pursuit of excellence, and they should also make it known that the organization will not accept mediocrity.

How does a leader accomplish that goal? First, ensure that everyone in the organization knows why excellence is necessary and that sustained performance is the goal. For example, consider when you take your automobile to get your brakes changed. You expect the mechanic to perform the complete brake job flawlessly. While his reputation and competence is important, you are more concerned that he performs his best work ever on your car. To take it one step further, if your brakes failed and you were in accident, his past accomplishment would mean nothing to you.

Just as with the mechanic, leaders must strive to ensure that everyone in the organization strives for excellence with every task. Leaders should work hard to create an environment where everyone is aware that a lack of concentration will often lead to a decrease in productivity. Performance can often be linked directly to the level of focus and concentration. Most of us have failed at something in our lives. When we reflected back for a reason for the failure, it was typically obvious that we were not focused enough on accomplishing that particular task. Often, the lack of focus is because we have become complacent.

Complacency will eventually lead to mediocre performance in the workplace. How does one avoid becoming complacent? While there is no simple or inclusive

1.   Quoted in *The Times of India* online, "Sacred Space," July 3, 2004. http:// timesofindia.indiatimes.com/articleshow/762827.cms

2.   *Ibid.*

answer, in order to ensure that complacency does not arise in the organization, leaders should be aware of two areas. Ensure standards and goals are not relaxed; remain energized and innovative.

Leaders must work hard to make sure that the pursuit of goals and enforcement of standards do not weaken over time. High standards in the workplace are paramount when meeting expectations and goals. Success in an organization can create an environment where people are relaxed.

Often, the first indicator of this is relaxation of standards being enforced. Dean Smith, the former basketball coach of the North Carolina Tarheels, is one of most successful coaches in the history of the game. One of his strengths was that he did not allow his players to get caught up in their success. Even though his teams won many more games than they lost, he always seemed more concerned about the team's executions rather than if they won or loss. He knew that, if he held his players accountable to a high standard of performance, winning would take care of itself. The principle in the constant concern of meeting expectations of high standards will produce outstanding results in any type of organization. It will also ensure that complacency does not work its way into the job.

Most people who reach a high level of accomplishment have a formula for success. In some cases, it might be their innovation or their work ethic. Maybe they take risks when they make decisions. Often, an indicator of complacency is when an individual goes away from the components that made him or her successful. For example, consider a supervisor whose strengths are his or her personal involvement with unit members and ensuring two-way communications. Once the section is successful, the supervisor may relax his or her communication. It is a fair assumption to state that, when the communication routine weakens, the performance will go with it. Productive individuals understand that success takes constant effort and complacency can lead to mediocrity.

Humility Indicates Strength

Humility is an important component of a productive leader's attitude. Others respect and enjoy being around someone who is successful yet stays modest. How does a leader display a humble attitude? While there is no exclusive answer, a leader can use three basic practices to help him or her stay humble and project humility:

Remember where you come from
Never stop learning
Keep results in perspective

Leaders should remember that their success came from sacrifice and hard work, not from being anointed. Humble leaders handle success with dignity and class. President George Washington came from humble beginnings. History shows that he never allowed himself to become arrogant or self-serving. In fact, his first inaugural speech was only six minutes long, making it the shortest inaugural speech in history. It exemplified his humble reluctance to accept such a high office while simultaneously showing his determination to serve the new country to the best of his ability.

Successful people are true to who they are and the principles they believe in. If success changes someone in a negative way, then he or she is not truly successful. Being humble is often viewed as a weakness when it can actually be a tremendous advantage. Humble leaders do not allow their own authority to blur their judgment. The leader who recognizes that mistakes are made creates an environment where others in the workplace feel comfortable taking risks and making errors occasionally.

History shows that individuals who possessed humility made some of the bravest decisions. Rosa Parks was known as a very humble woman. But on December 1, 1955, in Montgomery, Alabama, she changed the world by not giving her bus seat up to a white passenger. Just like many people before and after her, Rosa Parks proved that humility does not mean that an individual is weak.

A large part of an individual leadership style comes from personal past experiences. All humans are products of their environment to a great extent. Leaders are no exception to this. They should remain grounded in the principles that allowed them to become leaders.

Continue to Learn

A truly educated person never stops learning. One method of staying humble includes striving to gain knowledge.

Former First Lady Abigail Adams said, "Learning is not attained by chance; it must be sought for with ardor and attended to with diligence."[3]

Leaders have a responsibility to their organization to constantly learn and share their knowledge throughout the workplace. However, humility should be used when teaching, training, and giving feedback. No one desires to be talked to in manner that makes him or her feel incompetent. If sharing information is done with a sense of humility, it will be welcomed.

---

3.   Quoted in John Bartlett, *Bartlett's Familiar Quotations*, 17th edition, ed. Justin Kaplan (New York: Little, Brown and Co, 2002).

To ensure that information is shared with humility, follow the advice of Lord Chesterfield of Ireland. He said, "Never seem more learned than the people you are with. Wear your learning like a pocket watch, and keep it hidden. Do not pull it out to count the hours, but give the time when you are asked."[4]

People expect their leaders to create an environment where they can increase their knowledge and become a more productive performer. Nevertheless, leaders have a responsibility to deliver this educational environment with dignity and humility.

Results Are More than the Bottom Line

Results reign supreme in an organization; leaders must treat them as such. However, there is a fine line in the way that the institution should focus on results. If leaders use little humility and dignity when expressing their concerns about results, it could have a negative impact in the workplace. Most employees realize the bottom line for the organization is to be profitable and everyone in the workplace shares responsibility to ensure earnings are made. However, leaders are expected to accomplish organizational goals without treating others with the lack of dignity and humility that they deserve.

While the art of applying the right amount of concern on results is not an easy task to accomplish, it can be done with the proper attitude and approach. Results are the bottom line in an institution. Members of the organization and their actions determine if the goals are met or not. The leadership should concern themselves about results as well as the small accomplishments that are being fulfilled in order to achieve the desired goal. Rather than expending all of their energy and focusing on just the result, efficient leaders apply attention to every detail in the facet of the process. The process will drive the result in the long run.

A leader's attitude is the truest representation of who he or she is and what he or she believes in. People in any community will not always believe what they hear, but they will believe most of what they see and feel. If a leader strives to have an attitude that indicates he or she is professional, committed, passionate, and humble and will not become complacent, then others throughout the company will be happier and more productive.

In most organizations, the difference between being successful and mediocre is razor thin. It also can be directly related to the attitude of the organizational leadership. While it is true that one cannot control his or her environment, he or she can control his or her attitude. But when a leader chooses to react with the proper

4.   *Ibid.*

attitude, he or she will have a direct impact on the surrounding environment. So improve your attitude, and be a better leader.

PART III
Performance

8

It Is Judgment Day

Leaders are judged on performance. Whether it is sports, business, or the military, leaders are judged on their performance as it adds up to obtaining their end goal.

My favorite quote of author Ben Sweetland is, "Success is a journey, not a destination."[1] The same saying applies to obtaining successful performance within an organization. Desired performance does not simply happen. It is a process. Performance is the result of effort and planning.

Even though the word "performance" is easy to define as strong versus weak, performance is much more difficult to describe and achieve within an organization. Why? It is because performance can have many variables. For example, there is short- and long-term performance. Sometimes performance is very subjective, yet other times it is black-and-white. Achieving positive performance within a society is a process of fluidity. It must be treated with a flexible and visionary thought process.

An outstanding example of top performance in the workplace is Henry Ford's Model T automobile. In 1908, Ford produced the first Model T. The car became very popular because it was easy to drive and maintain. To keep up with the demand of the Model T, Ford created the first moving assembly line. Workers stood in place and installed parts as the car progressed down the line. Ford also designed a conveyor belt to deliver parts to the workers.

Potential Is Just a Promise

Leaders are assigned the responsibility of taking potential and molding it into performance. This is perhaps one of most difficult duties of a leader. There is one major reason that going from potential to performance is a very challenging task:

---

1.   Quoted in ThinkExist.com, "Sweetland, Ben." http://en.thinkexist.com/quotes/ben_sweetland/

a leader has little or no control over many of the components that impact positive results. For example, consider an injury to a superstar player. In the business world, consider a downturn in the economy.

Leaders should maximize their energy and efforts to control their workplace so they can make sound decisions concerning the events that they have control over. If a leader concentrates his or her efforts on things within the process that he or she cannot control, it is wasted time and effort. While contingency plans are effective and should be employed, a leader should spend most of his or her time and energy perfecting the course of action that is in place instead of worrying about things that are out of the company's control.

Making Others Better

Effective leaders find ways to enhance the performance of others. In the early stages of Michael Jordon's professional basketball career, he was known as a player who possessed great talent. He won the Rookie of the Year award in 1985 and the Player of the Year award in 1988. He also played several times in the NBA All-Star game. In 1991, he won his first of six NBA championships. With that first championship, not only did he prove himself as a great player individually, he proved he could also lead and motivate his teammates to reach their ultimate goal.

Oftentimes, leaders in the workplace are not graded on how they perform as individuals. They are evaluated on how their organization as a whole performs.

So how can leaders impact the performance of others? As I have discussed in the first two sections, communication and attitude are paramount to effective leadership. If you view communication as the foundation and attitude as the structure of a productive organization, then performance would be the exterior. The exterior is the first thing that is noticed. In most cases, it creates a lasting impression.

To be able to understand performance, leaders must first realize what their goal is. It sounds like an oversimplification, but no one can be expected to achieve something if it is unattainable or if the goal is not specific enough to be understood. In many cases, a leader's goals for performance are given to him or her. In this situation, the leader needs to ensure the goal is achievable and he or she has the available resources to be successful. If there is doubt about the task, then questions and research may be required. It is always more productive to ask questions initially instead of just blindly accepting a goal and then discovering later that the direction or intent of the objective was not understood. If a goal is not attainable, it should be viewed more as dream than an expectation. While high expectations are necessary and healthy for an organization, the expectations must be attainable. Just as parents factor in age-appropriate behavior before they set standards for their children, leaders must consider many factors before they endorse or set a goal for their organization. Unattainable goals can have a negative impact on morale throughout an organization.

Solid leaders realize that productive organizations are built on teamwork. I stated earlier that most people want to feel that they belong to something bigger than they are. In most cases, individuals will work extremely hard to succeed in the team concept if they believe their performance is enhancing the team performance.

Leaders should work to ensure that everyone in an organization feels like he or she is a key link to the success of the unit. A winner in a political race will commonly spend a lot of time thanking his or her staff and supporters for their efforts. While the candidate was the winner, he or she realized that he or she would not have been elected to the position without campaign contributors, individuals working the phone banks, and many others throughout the campaign working as a team.

9

Motivation Fuels Performance

Positive performance does not occur without motivated workers. It is a leader's responsibility to ensure his or her organization is motivated. Sometimes, the term "motivation" is used as a buzzword that sounds nice, but it is not practiced in the workplace. Motivation can be defined in a very simple way. Ensure workers begin their day challenged and end their day feeling a sense of accomplishment. For motivation to be successful, several actions must occur first. Individuals should feel like they are a valuable member of the organization. Members should feel challenges within their work and feel empowered within the organizational structure. Also, it is important that leaders do not overreact when trying to motivate others so as not to turn them off.

Personal Value and Hard Work

It is paramount for members to have a sense of value of themselves in the institution. Individual sense of value translates to commitment on the behalf of those within the organization to enhance performance. Leaders play a vital role in ensuring that members feel they have an important role of the performance that the organization yields. Hard work and sacrifice are a must in order to produce positive results. Being the example is pertinent when it comes to hard work within the organization. Leaders should not hesitate to get involved and perform tasks they are not expected to do. By doing this, a leader is sending the message that he or she will never expect anyone to do something they will not do themselves. This powerful message is often received with enthusiasm throughout the workplace.

Thomas Edison once said, "There is no substitute for hard work." He also said, "Genius is one percent inspiration and ninety-nine percent perspiration."[1]

---

1. Quoted in John Bartlett, *Bartlett's Familiar Quotations*, 17th edition, ed. Justin Kaplan (New York: Little, Brown and Co, 2002).

Most employees are willing to work hard for success of their organization, but they want to know that their effort is appreciated and making a difference. Leaders should ensure that every member of the organization realizes the importance of his or her work. In automobile racing, a race car commonly has the major sponsors' names advertised on the body of the vehicle. Also, decals of all of the associate sponsors are displayed on the car as well.

It is almost impossible for individuals in any organization to stay motivated unless their work gives them a sense of belonging.

Challenge, Define, and Motivate

For most people to remain motivated in the workplace, they must feel that their work is challenging them. Leaders play a significant role in motivating others through the medium of challenge performance. Leaders must ensure the assigned tasks will challenge individuals in such a manner that they come to work motivated. Most workers would like their daily objectives to demand a quality effort from them in order to be successful. Leaders must monitor work to ensure it does not become mundane. In many cases, boredom will set in, and the quality of work will suffer if members of an organization are not challenged enough.

It is vital that leaders first describe to each individual his or her role in the organization. Then, leaders should not downplay the importance of these individuals or put expectations on them that they cannot achieve.

Babe Ruth is one of the most recognizable names in baseball history. A member of the National Baseball Hall of Fame, Ruth is famous for hitting home runs. But many baseball fans are unfamiliar with Eddie Collins. He is also in the National Baseball Hall of Fame, but it is for entirely different reasons than Ruth. Collins hit singles and had a high batting average. He was an outstanding base stealer, and he was known as the best defensive second baseman of his era. Both Ruth and Collins played and contributed to teams that won the World Series. Both men were great performers during the same time period, but they contributed in different ways.

Solid leaders realize that, just as Ruth and Collins were different types of contributors, members of their own organization are different and have varied skill sets. It is the leader's responsibility to match individual skills to the role that best fits into assisting organizational success. Ruth's team did not expect him to steal bases or bunt, but Collins' leadership did not demand that he lead his team in belting home runs. Effective leaders define roles for the individual that will allow that individual's talents to improve the organization.

Leaders should ensure the working society consists of a climate that will assist the workers to meet challenges. When I was around twelve years old, I spent time doing things like hauling wood and rocks after school. Most of the time, I did these chores alone. I would hook the trailer to a tractor we had, and I would haul wood, rock, hay, or whatever needed to be done.

When I was finished, I would back the trailer into the shed to protect it from the bad weather. Backing a trailer can be a very difficult job, especially for a twelve-year-old boy. To steer the trailer left, I had to turn the wheels to the right.

I was not very good at backing the trailer into the shed. In fact, I dreaded it. On several occasions, I was trying to back the trailer into the shed, and I would oversteer. The trailer would get crossed up. Then I would have to move forward and try again. Just about when I was going to cry and give up, my Uncle Johnnie would show up. He lived very close to where the trailer was parked.

He would smile and say, "What's up, Ben? Is the tractor not behaving well today?"

Then he would help me park it correctly. The tractor seemed to drive differently when he was there to tell me when to turn to the left or right. After it was parked, he would give me a pep talk about how I was improving my backing techniques.

Now, when I reflect back on those days, I realize that my uncle was hiding out of sight the whole time I was struggling with that trailer. He knew I would never master the art of backing up the trailer if I did not challenge myself. Also, he knew that, if I got to the point of quitting, the trailer would have defeated me. My uncle was not going to allow that to happen.

Just like Uncle Johnnie, leaders should create an environment where challenges exist in the workplace, but plenty of support balances the challenges.

Showing Trust by Empowering

Empowerment is one of the soundest ways to motivate in the workplace. What are the keys for leaders to empower effectively? Leaders must have confidence in the members of their organization. Leaders must be more concerned with organizational success than with who received the credit. An environment must be created where empowerment can grow and gain momentum.

A leader's confidence in an individual can be instilled through that individual's training and past achievement. But the true proof of confidence is with action. During a recent flight, I was sitting next to a young man, a cameraman for a television show. He filmed things such as hunting and diving.

I asked, "What do you think about your work? What do you like? What do you dislike?"

He explained, "I feel more productive when I am given expectations and then trusted to accomplish the task."

I noticed he used the word "trusted" rather than "allowed." The feeling of being trusted is far more personal than being allowed to do something. Empowering is an ultimate sign of confidence and trust. I have associated with and heard of leaders who motivated and inspired others to a degree that most are not capable of doing. Those particular leaders possessed the "it" factor. People seemingly connect with a leader that they share a professional and personal relationship with the perfect mixture. In many cases, when a leader shows his or her confidence by trusting an individual to act with autonomy, there is a personal as well as professional exchange. This will often motivate the individual to focus and perform at much higher level than he or she would if he or she was just following directions.

Leaders Must Know When Acceptance Is Best

For a leader to show confidence in another, he or she must be willing to accept the end result. This does not mean a leader should accept performance that does not meet requirements. But he or she cannot get caught up in the one-upmanship game where he or she is constantly trying to add on or improve the idea or project.

One of my favorite children's books is *Guess How Much I Love You* by Sam McBratney, the story of two hares named Little Nutbrown Hare and Big Nutbrown Hare who love each other very much. Throughout the book, Little Nutbrown Hare tries many times to prove his feelings by doing actions like stretching his arms wide, hopping high, and standing on his toes. After each action, he tells Big Nutbrown Hare that he loves him that much.

Each time, Big Nutbrown Hare thanks the little fellow and then performs the exact same action. However, because he is bigger than Little Nutbrown Hare, Big Nutbrown Hare can do the action a little bit more than the younger hare can; for example, he can stretch his arms wider and hop a little higher. He explains that this is how much he loves Little Nutbrown Hare.

Even though the younger hare appreciates the love from Big Nutbrown Hare, he is a little melancholy that he is not able to express his love for Big Nutbrown Hare to the fullest extent. He keeps trying to find a way to express his love for Big Nutbrown Hare.

In the end, they are both lying under the stars, preparing for a night of sleep. Little Nutbrown Hare tells the older hare that he loves him all the way to the moon. This garners the response that he was hoping for from Big Nutbrown Hare, so Little Nutbrown Hare goes to sleep with a smile on his little rabbit face.

The elder hare does one last check on the young hare to ensure he is okay before he drifts off to sleep. He smiles at Little Nutbrown Hare and says, "I love you all the way to the moon ... and back."[2]

While this story could have several themes, I use it to illustrate that, when a leader realizes that someone has done his or her very best to accomplish a goal or task, the right response is to ensure that his or her confidence remains intact and accept his or her effort without adding much rebuttal.

---

2. Sam McBratney, *Guess How Much I Love You* (Cambridge, MA: Candlewick Press, 1994).

10

True Leaders Lead

Leaders who empower effectively understand that positive results are the goal. They are not usually concerned about who receives the credit. The message must be communicated clearly through the workforce. Nothing can squash motivation quicker than a leader taking or displacing the credit for a successful accomplishment. If credit or recognition is displaced, then a sense of betrayal—both on personal and professional level—could ripple throughout the workplace. People tend to leave most concerns about their jobs at work, but, if they feel the betrayal is serious enough to be taken personally, it will be on their minds at home. Often, it will eat away at them in an unhealthy manner. If not corrected, it will drain them of the spark that drives their motivation to perform at high levels. Displacement of recognition can be more devastating to junior members. They have yet to gain the experience that enables them to compartmentalize their thoughts, so their motivation is not negatively impacted.

Actions Often Speaks Louder than Words

Leaders should understand that motivating others requires more than just a fiery speech or some gimmick for a short-term gain. Organizational motivation works best when it is a process that is constructed to motivate and keep individuals galvanized over time.

I once talked with an eight-year-old girl named Catie about the attempt to motivate others into changing undesirable behavior to desired actions.

She explained, "When my friends treat me in a way that I think is wrong and makes me angry, I write them letters." She continued, "In my letters, I am very direct. I tell them how mean and immature they were. I tell them that I would never speak to them again if they did not apologize."

I asked, "Do your friends apologize?"

She responded, "I never send the letters. I just tear them into little pieces."

Puzzled, I asked, "Why?"

She explained, "By writing the letters, I feel better because it eases my bitter feelings toward my friends. But, at the same time, it doesn't hurt anyone." She continued, "After everyone calmed down, we would discuss the problem and remain friends."

Smiling, I asked, "How do you start each letter?"

Chuckling, she responded, "Dear Nincompoop."

Like Catie, leaders must realize that sometimes the best motivation is to allow the process time to work.

Nothing Is Free

In any organization, resources are imperative to positive performance. Resources can be broken down into two categories: physical and mental. On the physical side, leaders must ensure that workers have the tools needed to be successful. No one would attempt to travel three thousand miles across the country on a trip in an automobile with the resources for a five-hundred-mile trip.

While my grandfather was not the first to make this statement, he would often say, "You cannot get blood out of a turnip."

Nothing can be more demoralizing for workers than to be expected to accomplish a task without the necessary means to do so. To remain productive, leaders must always search for ways to achieve the maximum success. They must ensure their organization has the resources to achieve its goal while not wasting them.

Mental resources do not deal with one's IQ. Rather, they involve the thought processes chosen to accomplish goals. I watched a series of documentary shows on television about the history of companies. It included examples from the food to the airline industries. The show extensively discussed how the companies were founded and succeeded. It also talked about their struggles and the methods that were incorporated to build them into giants of their industry. Clearly, the companies were prospering as a result of leadership that was taking a proactive stance concerning decisions that dealt with change and meeting the customer's desires. However, when certain events occurred, such as competition, change, or recession, the organization became stagnant. Leadership reacted in a defensive manner. The results were negative, and their organization suffered. Also, it was obvious that, when a positive turnaround occurred, it would be in direct correlation with being proactive with their decision-making process.

It All Comes Down to the Leader

While reaching and maintaining organizational performance includes components like understanding goals and motivating others, most successful leaders share a personal component. It is a mind-set that defines who they are.

Several years ago, I went to pick up my dad from his workplace. It was just a few days before he retired. As he walked from his work structure, he glanced back several times with a disappointed look on his face. His actions did not surprise me. While he had talked about how much he was looking forward to the day he would retire, I knew he had mixed emotions about it.

Once he got in the car, I asked, "How do you want your co-workers to remember you?"

Smiling, he responded, "I want them to say that I worked hard and performed my job well. I want them to remember that my actions caused others to work hard and perform well."

Meaningful leaders put the "P" in CAP by taking their personal convictions and work ethics to motivate others throughout their organization in achieving the organizational goals.

Conclusion

Dear Reader,

I hope that you found this book informative and that you can apply these messages in your daily life. I hope it was humorous and interesting in a way that caused you to smile and that made the reading enjoyable. I hope you found it thought provoking in a way that caused you to challenge yourself to be a better leader within your organization. If I have met any of the three goals, it was well worth my time and effort. Thank you, and good luck as you put a CAP on your leadership style.

978-0-595-47616-9
0-595-47616-3